The Heroes Quilt
2020

An embroidered

patchwork quilt

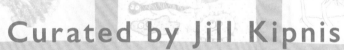

Curated by Jill Kipnis

Jill Kipnis *Inspirational Embroidery*

An embroidered patchwork quilt

I started 2020 on a boat with my husband sailing down the River Thames in London. We were looking forward to the new year ahead. Little did we know then there was going to be a pandemic, caused by a newly discovered coronavirus, and how it would change 2020 and many years to come. We would all have to adapt and, at the time of writing this, try to find a new normal.

We were hearing on the news about some virus in Asia that was causing concern. We watched the news, and felt that as it was a problem in Asia, we wouldn't be affected by it. How wrong we were.

On 16 March 2020, Matt Hancock, Secretary of State for Health and Social Care, told the UK House of Commons that all unnecessary social contact should cease. On 23 March Boris Johnson, the UK Prime Minister, announced a total lockdown to help reduce the spread of the virus. Now we were part of that pandemic and everyone was worried that the wonderful National Health Service (NHS) would be overwhelmed, so we were told to stay at home, work from home, wash our hands, and stay two metres apart to help contain the virus.

Businesses and schools closed immediately. Only essential shops were allowed to remain open and home-schooling became a reality. While some people, like myself, loved having our children at home, others with younger children found it more challenging. In adapting to this new way of life perhaps we learnt to appreciate teachers, and other essential workers, a little more. People were worried as the death toll started to rise and we became aware of the side-effects of the virus.

The NHS was key to everything. We witnessed staff becoming exhausted and falling ill, with some even making the ultimate sacrifice. The NHS workers kept us going through that stressful time. Now, as I write, they stand ready to support us again. Although we are better prepared this time, it is still not easy. Staff will be dealing with all the ongoing issues people have, such as cancer, strokes and diabetes, at the same time as treating patients with the Covid-19 coronavirus.

This is why we are dedicating this book to the NHS workers and to all those who passed away due to the coronavirus. For each book sold, we'll be making a contribution to 'NHS Charities Together' – the official charity linked to the NHS which supports over 240 NHS charities across the UK. The role of NHS charities is to provide the added extras for staff, volunteers and patients that are not covered by core NHS funding.

If you would like further details, please look at the NHS Charities Together blog which has frequent updates on the additional benefits it provides. ***www.nhscharitiestogether.co.uk/blog/***

£5.00 from the sale of this book will be donated to NHS Charities Together
(registered charity no. 1186569)

How this project came about

I have always been fascinated by the power of stitch and the historical meaning it can have.

Like everyone else, I was trying to find a new routine during the lockdown. I was missing my embroidery teaching. I created ideas and busily posted designs on social media to try and inspire people to get creative with embroidery. I sat out in my garden and so enjoyed my embroidery. It took my mind into a relaxing, peaceful place, but I missed the interaction with like-minded people. A few weeks into lockdown, I was contacted by one of my students, Sue Arran, who attended my regular embroidery classes. Sue, like me, wanted to try and come up with something that brought people together through embroidery; to create something during the crisis. I have always been moved by a historical patchwork piece that I stumbled across at the Royal Festival Hall on the South Bank, London a few years ago. This amazing patchwork quilt was created for the Festival of Britain Exhibition of 1951 and was embroidered by a group of women from Twickenham in Surrey, England.

They embroidered 100 squares; each square represented something to do with a year from 1851 to 1950. These ladies created some beautifully embroidered squares showing inventions, illustrations of war, people who had made an impact over the century. I always found this piece of work very powerful. There in front of me was a historical document of 100 years all illustrated in stitch.

I have a student who has been coming to me for several years, making three patchwork quilts for her children out of their old clothes. She carefully stitched the pieces together and each stitch carried love and memories. She wanted her children to keep these quilts as a happy memory of their times together; they will be with them for the rest of their lives.

Also, I was privileged to be asked to supply some materials for a beautiful quilt that a mother was making for a school pupil who had lost a parent to Covid-19. The mother organised all the girls in the year to embroider a message to their friend on a square from their own school skirts. They created an amazing quilt that will encase the child with the love and support that she so needs at this terrible time.

When Sue called me, everything came together. Suddenly it was clear: let us create a quilt that everyone and anyone could contribute to. We wanted people to embroider their 'hero' on a square during the lockdown and write a short paragraph explaining their choice. The 'hero' did not have to be a person; it could be an object or situation. Our only stipulation was the square had to be 20cm × 20cm (8in × 8in).

We wanted to create something memorable and historical together to show the power of stitch.

I publicised the project on social media and, before we knew it, people from all over the world were sending us squares. Friends and people whom we had never met were trusting us with their beautiful squares and emotional stories.

We now have a fantastic quilt. It has taken us six months to put together and, ironically, I sewed the last stitch in the quilt the night before the start of the second national lockdown. Thank you to all the amazing people who sent us squares. We have together created something truly amazing. I hope future generations will look at this quilt, read the stories and understand what we went through.

Jill Kipnis, November 2020

How the quilt was made

Sue and I knew we wanted to create a large quilt, to have impact and meaning. When we started we had no idea how many squares we would receive or if the quilt would work.

We received a few squares within weeks of advertising the idea. We were amazed at how people heard about us. We had squares from America, Spain, Germany and all over the UK.

When the squares started to arrive, we never knew what the story was going to say; some made you laugh, some made you cry. Each story was so moving and meaningful.

We decided to call a halt to all contributions towards the end of September, when we had almost 50 squares. We intended to sew the squares next to one another, but each square was so unique we felt we had to add a border around each one, to better display their individuality. So we added a quilted border around each square.

We started with arranging the squares in a large space. It was so difficult to decide which square went where. We had to look at the colour and fabric balance. We started to sew and realised after six hours that the layout wasn't right, but after some unpicking and re-arranging, we got there.

The quilt took over the Kipnis kitchen for almost a month. When we started the project, we thought, come the autumn, the virus would be under control so we could ask a local sewing group to help us put this masterpiece together. But infection rates were starting to increase and although we were not in official national lockdown, we had a ban on households mixing. Putting the quilt together took me almost four weeks of stitching from morning to evening. It was quite challenging to keep lines straight and towards the end too difficult to manage under a sewing machine. But at last it was done and we are now so pleased with this fantastic historical document that we've all created.

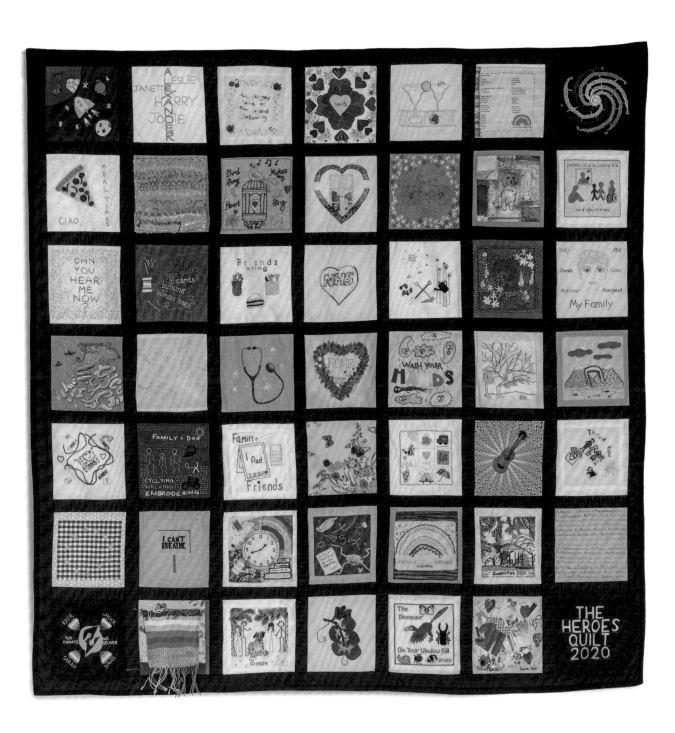

Lockdown April 2020

My sewing class went online. We are a group of ladies sewing 36 squares, tutored by our own talented Lucy. Each square represented something to be grateful for.

My patch for the Heroes Quilt is a selection from those 36 squares.

Morning sun – a new day.

A cup of tea – memories.

Deliveries – keeping in touch.

Bees – hmm hmm hmm.

Music – singing and dancing.

Flowers – beautiful earth.

Honey – on toast.

Rainbows – looking forward.

My sewing during Covid-19 has kept me in touch and busy!

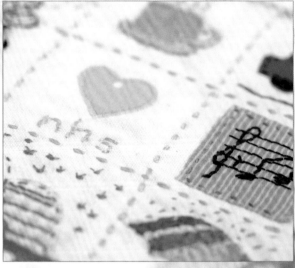

Pat Robinson, Nottinghamshire, UK

Hand embroidered using stranded cotton. Appliqué with running, chain, long and short, back and lazy daisy stitches.

You donate, we deliver

A friend of mine (Katie) received a text message from another friend, a nurse working during the earliest days of the pandemic, who could not leave the ward to get something to eat as they were so busy. The canteens were closed. This led to a fantastic effort on the part of Katie, her mum Jackie and friends Sarah and David, to make and deliver meals to local hospitals. At its height, they were delivering over 2000 meals, made possible by people's donations and the goodwill of the helpers, including family members, professional chefs and an army of drivers.

This struck me as a brilliant example of how people pulled together to help one another in this unique situation. Katie, Jackie, Sarah and David devoted many hours and boundless energy to make life more bearable for the hard-working NHS staff.

Sue Arran, London, UK

Hand embroidered using stranded cotton and metallic thread. Long and short, back and stem stitches used, and rows of satin stitches.

My cycle ride

Time away from the television headlines.

Nature continues.

Trees show their new lime-green shoots.

Birds are busy making nests.

Swallows return from their winter migration.

Bluebells cover the forest floor.

Pheasants' cries tell me they are looking for
a mate.

Horses look at me from their stable door.

Wisps of bright green shoots are just appearing
in the farmer's field.

Hawthorn trees laden with white blossom.

All this in just an hour of exercise.

(Well don't tell anyone: my cycle ride takes just a
little longer!)

Paula Bradbury, London, UK

Hand embroidered using stranded cotton. Lazy daisy stitch used for the flowers and the bicycle has been machine embroidered.

A lace rainbow

A lace rainbow has so many levels of meaning.

A rainbow has a wider meaning of harmony in diversity and hope. During Covid-19 the rainbow is a symbol of hope; many children drew rainbows and put them up in windows, showing support and unity with the national heart and key workers and each other.

This is based on a design by Lou Woo. I used the coloured threads I had, different colours, not all the same weight. Some I had for a long time, some newly acquired; some came to hand quickly, some I had to hunt for, some turned up in unexpected places. I could have bought the kit with new threads, but I used what I had. The rainbow isn't perfect as life isn't perfect. The crystal beads in the rainbow show that we need rain as well as sunshine to create something beautiful; the beads also seem to represent the tears of so many people who have suffered a loss at this terrible time. There is a Dorset button in the middle to signify the sunshine, the warm weather we experienced in April and May 2020 and the sunshine that will return to people's lives in the future. Stormy days don't last forever. It is mounted on a piece of my late husband Peter's polo shirt which is special to me, and also the only black material I could find in my stash!

I find lace making is a rhythmic meditation offering a retreat from the buffeting of everyday life. I enjoy choosing which bobbins to use, some new, some old, that friends have bought for me at different times in my life, some given by friends or made for me by family. Some are beautifully painted, some are functional but no less beautiful or meaningful.

A rainbow is simply bright, colourful and cheerful and I hope it brightens up the day for others.

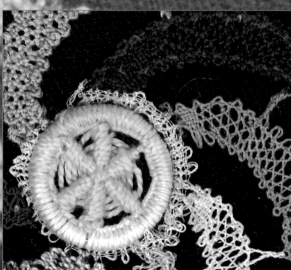

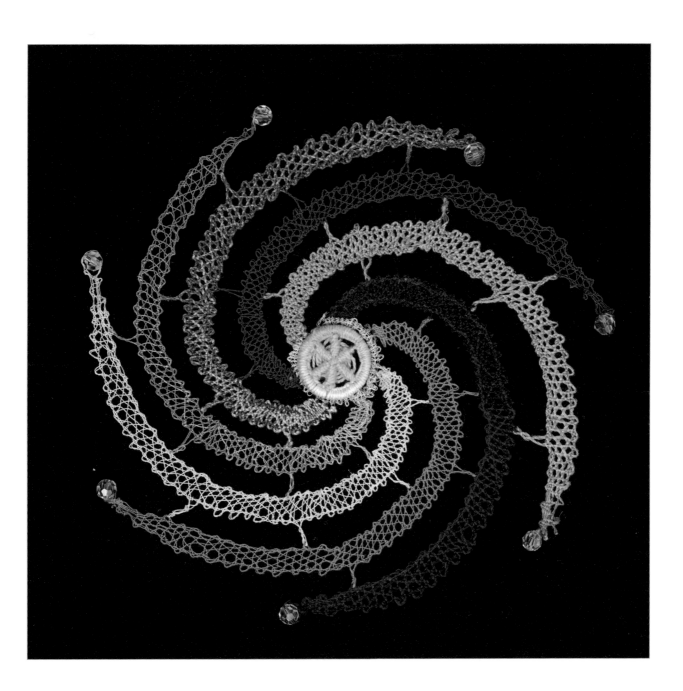

Kathy Stearne, Wiltshire, UK

Handmade lace pieces, creating a wonderful rainbow with a Dorset button made for the centre, finished with some beautiful crystal beads.

The island getaway

My lockdown hero is the Nintendo game 'Animal Crossing: New Horizons'.

My daughters bought it for me for Mothers' Day and it's truly delightful – you get your own little island, complete with sweet animal villagers, which you can decorate as you like. You can spend your days fishing, catching insects or simply watching the tides roll in and out. Best of all, you can visit friends' islands. We've spent many happy family hours exploring islands together. It even made it possible for us to virtually spend time with my partner's daughter, who lives a long way away and we haven't been able to see her in person for months. It's been a vital escape from stressful times. There is a hidden message in the writing in my piece; the letters of the word 'animal' are picked out in blue and our initials in green.

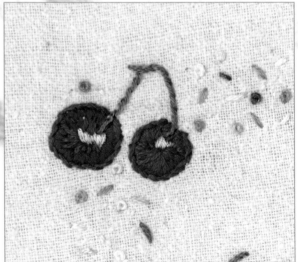

we stayed
home on
our island
getaway

Hannah Lawrence, London, UK

Hand embroidered using stranded cotton. Seeding, lazy daisy, cross, satin and stem stitches used.

SpaceX

I have been studying for my astrophysics university exams during the lockdown, which has kept me sane and given me something to do!

I was also really excited to watch the SpaceX launch from Florida which took place during the lockdown, which inspired me to do this piece.

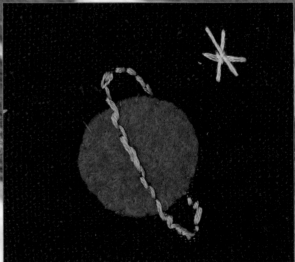

Phoebe Kipnis, London, UK

Hand embroidered using stranded cotton and sewing threads. Appliqué with stab, straight and long and short stitches.

The scrub hub

I was so pleased and inspired when I heard about the idea for this quilt. It was a perfect way of relaxing and planning a design centred on our scrub hub set up in Wandsworth with Alice and her team. I had been enjoying great classes the previous year at the Royal School of Needlework up in the attics at Hampton Court, so it was a perfect sampler of some of the stitches I had learnt. I even contacted my American stitching pal who came over twice to join us. Combining scrub bags and quilt squares was pure therapy.

Gini Chappell, London, UK

Appliqué with hand stitching, using stranded cotton. Couching and gold jap used, as well as french knots, stem, straight and trellis filling stitches. Ribbon flowers also feature.

Sewing for Kingston

I began sewing hearts for S4K (Sewing for Kingston) to give to Covid-19 victims and their families. I started to do this because I wanted to do something to help in some way, to feel like something good and positive could come from an awful situation.

Greta Pollard, London, UK

Appliqué with hand stitching, running stitch in gold thread with the writing in stem stitch.

Waves, sky and mountains

Living in North Wales, with the sea on the doorstep and surrounded by mountains and forests, was a real blessing during this difficult time. Every afternoon I walked to the beach with my husband, daughter and our dog Luna.

The lockdown meant very sad days in the town, as the region is a tourism area, so seeing it empty and almost everything closed was a shock to us.

From those awful days, I keep only the lovely memories: the waves, sky, mountains far away, my family playing on the sand.

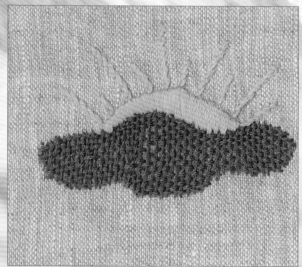

Silvia Ewing, Wales, UK

Hand embroidered using stranded cotton. Stitches used are trellis filling, chain, stem, seeding, satin, french knots and herringbone.

Friends

My heroes during the 2020 lockdown were the lovely friends who brought flowers, shopping and cake, all delivered to my door at a safe distance.

They certainly brightened my life.

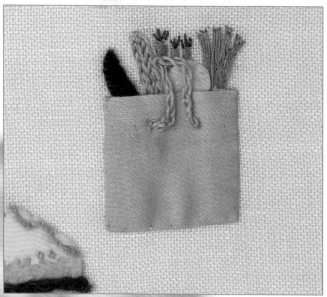

Wendy Chrichley, London, UK

Hand embroidered using stranded cotton. Appliqué and french knots, stem, lazy daisy, chain and straight stitches used.

Inside of the box

I've really enjoyed the Heroes Quilt project as it's made me think 'inside of the box' of my home environment while in this crazy lockdown time!

I've shared lockdown with fellow household members Alexander, Jodie, Harry and husband Leslie. It's been crazy, noisy, busy, quiet, lonely and emotional at different times.

Janette Paster, Hertfordshire, UK

Hand embroidered using stranded cotton and stem stitch.

Caring for all and my family

My medical studies were definitely my saviour during the lockdown, as they gave me direction and focus during the challenging period.

My embroidery alludes to this, but I also think the stethoscope symbolises the importance of caring for one another. Listening to the fears of friends and family requires us to slow down and be attentive in order to recognise vulnerability.

I hope this is a way of life that can be adopted in a post-Covid world.

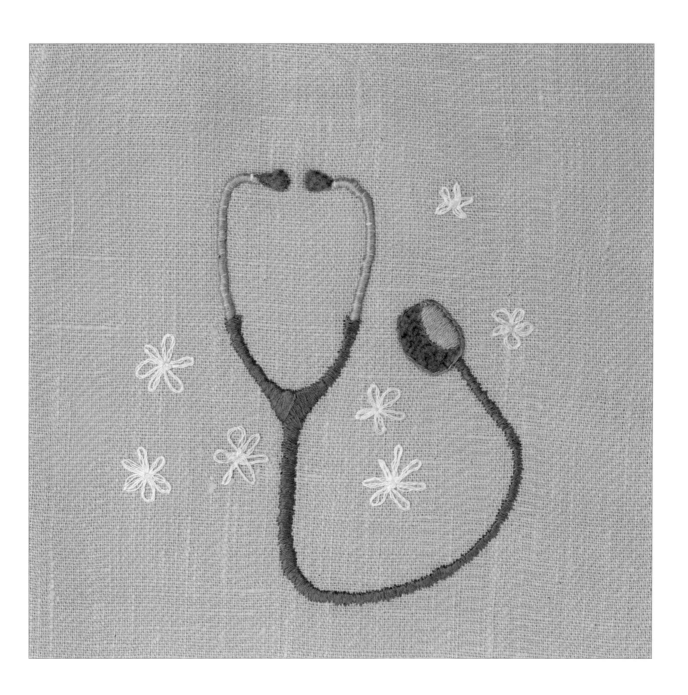

Sophie Bettis, London, UK

Hand embroidered using stranded cotton. Padded satin stitch with string padding and satin and lazy daisy stitches used.

Sewing before Covid-19, during the lockdown and after

Apart from my wonderful family, my sewing machine has been my constant companion during the Covid-19 crisis.

Self-employed, I would normally be busy making costumes for the West End theatres, English National Ballet and the Royal Ballet. With all these venues having to close and finding myself without any work, I swapped sequins for 'Scrubs4NHS', helping my local group sew much needed scrubs and scrubs bags for local hospitals, hospices and GP surgeries.

I just kept sewing to keep me sane!

I made face masks for many friends and family, bunting which I made for our VE day celebrations, as well as lots of handmade cards to send lockdown birthday wishes.

Tanya Mould, Surrey, UK

↘ *Hand embroidered with stranded cotton and metal threads, using running, couching and straight stitches.*

My NHS heart

During the lockdown I started cross-stitch to relax outside of my work hours as I wanted to reduce my screen time. I came across Lucy Martine's NHS embroidery challenge on Instagram and decided I wanted to give it a go.

I am looking forward to continuing this hobby and learning more techniques beyond lockdown, but I am so glad that my piece can live on beyond Instagram.

Chloe Marks, London, UK

Hand embroidered using stranded cotton with beads and chain stitch.

I see you

I've been thinking about the invisible versus visible during the lockdown. There are millions of people shielding who have been invisible from society. There are also those who are not deemed 'vulnerable' who nevertheless still have challenges of their disability to navigate in a world that is not inclusive at the best of times. Often their supportive equipment/person is more visible than they are.

This is why certain elements of the piece are red as opposed to the invisible people. These people have their own strategies which may have become impossible during the crisis, e.g. ongoing medical care, shopping home delivery, etc. These people are invisible to the Government. This current isolation may be similar to what some of the invisible are used to, but it does not lessen the sense of loss caused by missing out on our 'little wins'.

To anyone else who feels invisible: 'I see you'.

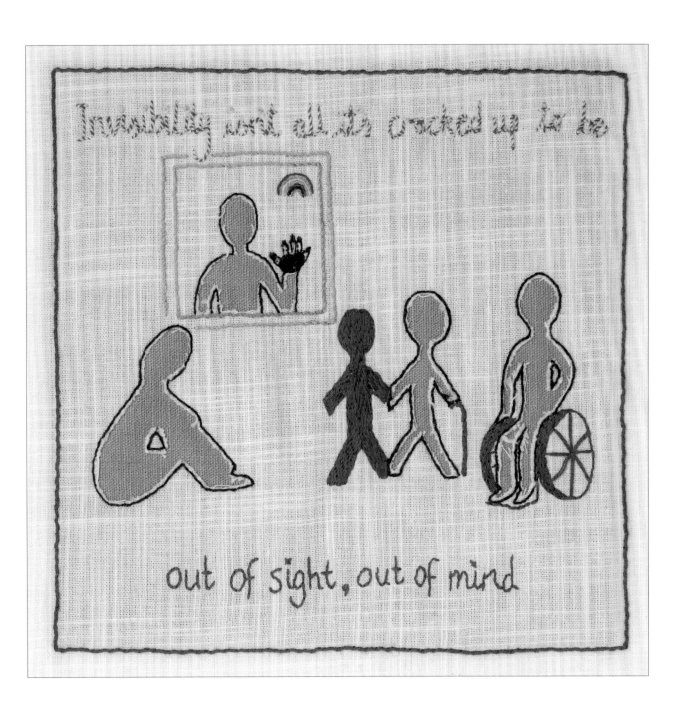

Jo Butler, West Yorkshire, UK

Hand embroidered using reverse appliqué and stranded cotton. Whipped back, back and long and short stitches used.

Gardening and the outdoors has kept a lot of people sane

In March 2020, I followed the Government's directive given to the 'old and vulnerable' and went into self-isolation. The TV was awash with news of panic buying, and empty shelves (where did all those toilet rolls go?) and there was a huge demand for supplies delivered to our doors. The world was in chaos.

In my isolation, I became a 'silver surfer,' using the internet, and sending emails to 'keep in touch' – something I thought I'd never get used to.

I also found solace in my beautiful garden. As Audrey Hepburn said, 'To plant a garden is to believe in tomorrow.' I spent hours potting up, pruning, planting and digging. Friends and family stepped in to help me with supplies and, in return, I gave them seedlings and vegetable plants so they too could start growing.

My Covid companion, loyal throughout, was a friendly robin. He would follow me around the garden, keeping me company all through the lockdown. One day he studied me for quite some time, with his head tilted in deep contemplation. Eventually, he flew at me – to gently remove a small bug from my hair!

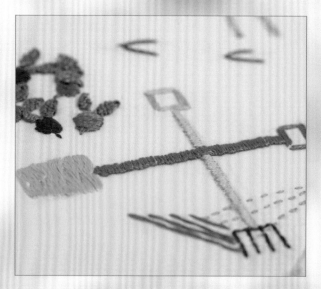

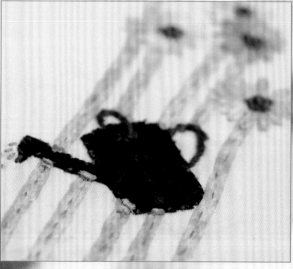

Kate Harvey, Devon, UK

Hand embroidered using stranded cotton. Appliqué with picots, lazy daisy, straight, blanket and couching stitches used.

I can't breathe

I wanted to stitch something to commemorate those campaigning and putting in the work to dismantle racism, those unpicking the historical structures that perpetuate it, exposing the corruption and toxicity that enabled it. The heroes in this are many, but the focus is the same. It's time for the world (especially myself and others in the white community) to own up to confronting the past and to put in the work to cultivate a future where no person is treated differently because of the colour of their skin.

I chose to replicate a placard seen at the London Black Lives Matter protests leading on from the unjustifiable death of George Floyd at the hands of the police. It celebrates those out there fighting, educating and protesting for change.

Brekke Friend, Norwich, UK

Hand embroidered using stranded cotton. Straight and back stitches used.

Baci the hero

The patchwork of mostly hand dyed or mono printed fabrics represents our fields where I have spent the last 12 weeks shielding. I would normally be caring for between 5 and 15 dogs in my boarding kennels where my little English springer, Baci, is my 'redcoat'. She too is missing her friends. My workmate and companion, she has made this lockdown bearable. Sadly, she is too naughty to be allowed in my studio.

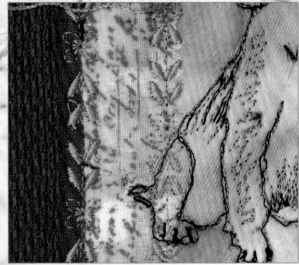

Jill Hill, East Anglia, UK

Hand dyed fabrics used to make a collage piece with lace. Machine embroidered motif and stitches from the sewing machine used to complete the square.

Generous friends and neighbours

We lost the first lot of tomato plants to a late frost. I complained a lot and soon our lovely friends and neighbours were leaving replacements on the doorstep.

We've been lucky to have all three boys home for lockdown, a rare treat. They've all helped in the garden and we've enjoyed the sun.

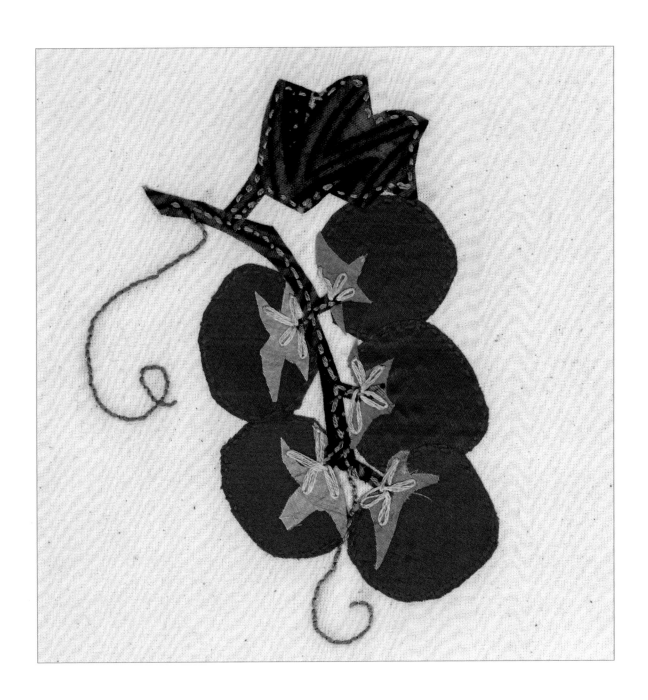

Nicola McCahill, Essex, UK

Hand embroidered with stranded cotton. Appliqué with running and lazy daisy stitches used.

A disconnected daisy chain

My square has significance to me for two reasons. The daisy chain isn't connected because I have felt isolated from my friends and family – especially with my Mom in Cape Town and my sister in Australia.

However, the flowers are also representative of nature and the beauty of peony season (which has occupied a lot of my time). That they go in a circle also shows how time will continue on, and nature will renew itself.

Lucy Hook, Kent, UK

Hand embroidered using stranded cotton. Lazy daisy and running stitches used.

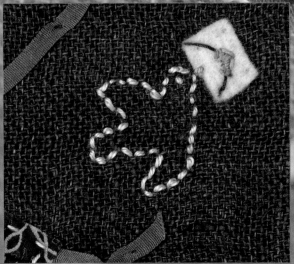

My friends, face masks and charity

My friends who kindly contributed to my Covid-19 charity project are my heroes. Thanks to them, I am donating the proceeds from the sale of my handmade masks to charity.

I was pleased to use my Savile Row apprenticeship skills which I hope can be seen in the quality of my masks.

Also, my friends' kind comments about the masks very much lifted my spirit and energy during this challenging time.

My quilt includes miniature masks made from the same fabric as the masks I sold.

The translation of the Japanese words embroidered here are:

> 'How are you? I am sending you a mask. Please be safe, Ryoko'.

Ryoko Manaka, London, UK

Appliqué and ribbons are couched down with straight, chain and running stitches.

The palo verde tree

I noticed the palo verde tree in the local CVS pharmacy parking lot as I was waiting in the drive-through line to pick up a prescription. I photographed it and, since the two upward reaching branches seemed to be bowing, decided to use it as my image for a contribution to the Heroes Quilt 2020, to express gratitude to our personal heroes of this pandemic.

A thank you card made from a photo of the square will let the workers at CVS know I value their help and that they are included in those being honoured by the quilt.

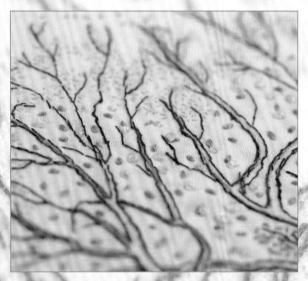

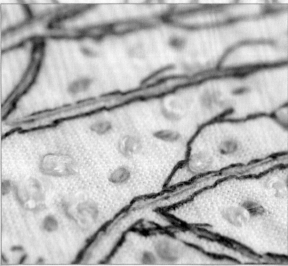

Kathleen Oettinger, Las Vegas, USA

Hand embroidered using stranded cotton and metallic threads. French knots, straight, back and seeding stitches used.

Thank you technology

These items have been my lifeline. I am undergoing treatment for Stage 4 cancer. My children (twins) are in Australia and New Zealand with my five grandchildren.

FaceTime and the phone have certainly kept my spirits up. I feel sure that it will have done the same for so many.

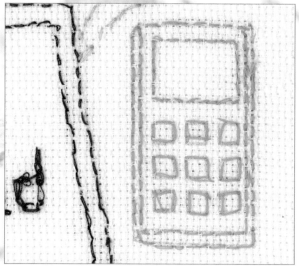

Pat Young, Yorkshire, UK

Hand embroidered on Aida cloth using stranded cotton. Back stitch and stem stitches used.

Gideon

Our lockdown experience has been overwhelmingly positive so far, giving us the opportunity to spend almost a full summer with our grown-up son and daughter, who otherwise would have still been at university, working in summer jobs, or on holiday with their friends. Luckily, we managed to stay safe and healthy, and the long summer days at home gave us a chance to deepen family ties and enjoy each other's company – playing games in the garden, making cocktails together, watching films, reading, laughing and relaxing.

At the very heart of our family during this time was Gideon, our handsome, funny, loving, two-year-old Irish wolfhound. He gave us a focus, and a reason for going out, every single day.

Notwithstanding the queues, the shortages, the hardships many people faced and the constant sanitising, my abiding memory of lockdown is of long morning walks in Trent Park woods with my husband and Gideon – and sometimes the kids, if it wasn't too early. We sometimes stopped halfway round to sit on a fallen tree dappled with sunshine, sipping a lovely hot coffee.

For a few precious hours a day, the pandemic seemed a world away.

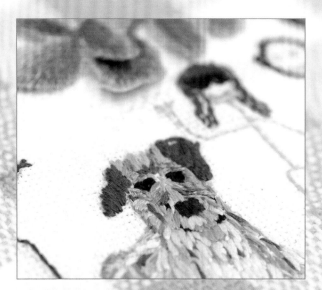

Jill Collins, London, UK

Hand embroidered on Aida fabric with appliqué machine embroidered leaves. Stranded cotton used with running, back and straight stitches.

My view

My friend and mentor Jill Kipnis embroidered a rainbow heart on her T-shirt.

I adapted the design and made greetings cards. This was very therapeutic and enjoyable during the lockdown.

Being confined to my first floor flat, this is the view from my french windows.

Wendy Chrichley, London, UK

Hand embroidered using stranded cotton and a variety of stitches: lazy daisy, stem, straight and french knots. Beautiful hand painted picture for the window scene, which is then embroidered over the top.

Ciao

Mealtimes have been such a saviour for me in lockdown. A time when the family comes together and shares good food has been the best thing to come out of it. As we all have more time at the moment, I have especially loved making the foods I treasure the most from scratch.

Italian is my favourite cuisine and so I decided to embroider a pizza slice with the vibrant green hue of a bell pepper. The confetti serves as a celebratory symbol, not only to celebrate the food I love, but also to shine a light on the collective power of cooking, which has been such a source of happiness for me during this incredibly difficult and challenging period.

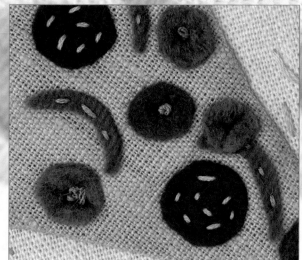

Annabel Kipnis, London, UK

Hand embroidered using stranded cotton and appliqué. Felt has been applied to decorate the pizza slice.
French knots, seeding and stem stitches used.

Lockdown litany

On 23 March 2020, the United Kingdom was placed in lockdown to prevent the spread of Covid-19 and to stem a rising tide of cases. At first it felt surreal, as unanticipated 'free time' combined with restrictions on activities, removed the structure of daily life. As the days passed, I watched as we created a new order out of chaos. Friends and family timetabled their lives to cope with the stay-at-home situation. My life evolved into an almost daily routine of gardening, sewing and reading, which brought calm reassurance that 'this too shall pass'.

The quilt square is titled 'Lockdown Litany – read, grow, sew, repeat' and shows a central clock representing time passing, three quarters depicting my hobbies and a rainbow quarter symbolising hope.

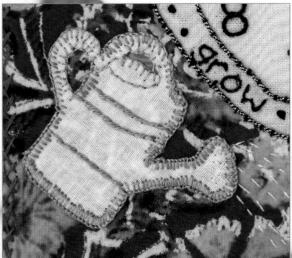

Chris Fraser, Hertfordshire, UK

The square shows a variety of techniques, threads and stitches. Appliqué in several places using metal and stranded cotton. Stitches used include lazy daisy, stem, blanket, french knots, seeding and couching.

The Queen's Park bandstand

My embroidery is of the bandstand in Queen's Park, London NW6. I have been lucky to live opposite the park for 25 years and it means a great deal to me. Our three children grew up playing there and it's where we walk our wee dog, Robbie.

Somehow during the lockdown, Queen's Park's Manager Richard Gentry and his team kept the park gates open for the benefit of us all. I am so grateful to Richard. His wife Celia is a good friend and the best baker I know. All through the lockdown she baked cakes for the park staff and every single Saturday would turn up at my door with delicious home baking for my family. I am so grateful to her.

My friend Lizzie Barker is a fitness trainer who has put me through my paces beside the bandstand for some years now. We have a lot of fun and she kept me fit throughout lockdown, come rain or shine, always lifting my spirits. I am grateful to her, too.

The bandstand is for me a symbol of friendship, support and good times. Richard, Celia and Lizzie: this is a tribute to each of you.

Susan Pym, London, UK

Hand embroidered using stranded cotton. French knots, blanket and straight stitches used.

My children and me

Lockdown gave us time and space to try new things. I bought a small loom a while ago but hadn't had a chance to use it. Keyworker rainbows brightened our days and reminded us all to be thankful, so it was the obvious choice – with the grey cloud of Covid underneath. We have been extremely grateful to our lovely community, friends and family, the local shop, the postal service and supermarket who have delivered everything we needed during the five months we were at home shielding.

My patch combines old with new, incorporating material I liberated during an early lockdown clear-out – another national trend as we sought to take control of our immediate surroundings and attempted to turn living spaces into offices and classrooms. The pattern captures the blue skies and nature that we appreciated so much as we adjusted to the 'new normal'. I have never heard the birds sing as loudly as they did this spring while there was no traffic for them to compete with.

I wanted to capture some of the feelings I had at the early stages of the pandemic, the sense of time passing and things shifting as the weeks went by. Perceptions changed so much, as well as the news.

On re-reading the poem, I thought I had made an error repeating a word, but no, food really had become an obsession. If we weren't cooking or eating, we were writing lists and planning where we could get hold of flour and various staples. The local shop, friends and the supermarket delivery were very much our heroes!

This summer we have welcomed chickens to the household and built vegetable beds and a greenhouse. We are far from self-sufficient, but it feels good to be producing at least some of our food.

The kids (aged 6 and 7 at lockdown) have been absolute heroes during these strange times. They have accepted the enormous shift in lifestyle in the six months they have been out of school and kept us going with their relentless good humour and endless play. Our attempts at home education started well but fizzled out as we tried to balance working from home with schooling and staying healthy and cheerful. Despite missing their friends, they have enjoyed us all being at home together and trying new things, especially arts and crafts. I enjoyed teaching them things I remember from my childhood.

My great-grandmother embroidered beautifully, and as her husband died of flu in 1918 it felt poignant picking up a needle and thread. I cannot claim to have mastered embroidery, but it has been comforting to try different crafts, and it has brought back childhood memories of learning to stitch with my grandma.

Lockdown has been a time of reflection; I feel we have caught a glimpse of how life might have been when there were fewer choices but maybe more time. I have come to appreciate how busy our lives are, and how many hours these skills, such as embroidery, take to perfect.

My great-grandparents were married in New York in 1915 and my grandma was born in Pennsylvania just over a year later. The *Pittsburgh Gazette Times* reported the city's first case of influenza on 1 October 1918, and my great-grandfather died 22 days later. Although I have heard parts of this story since I was a child, it is only now that I can start to imagine the shock, fear, and loss that my great-grandmother, and so many others, experienced.

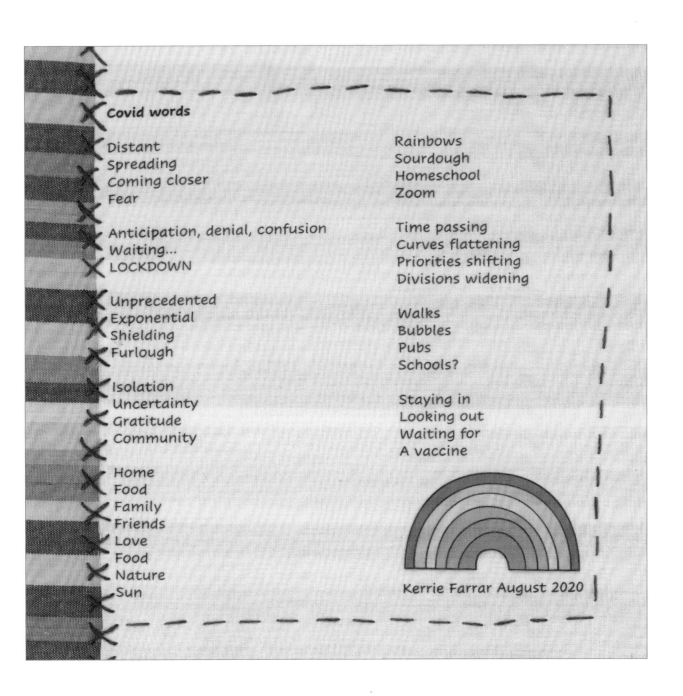

Covid words

Distant
Spreading
Coming closer
Fear

Anticipation, denial, confusion
Waiting...
LOCKDOWN

Unprecedented
Exponential
Shielding
Furlough

Isolation
Uncertainty
Gratitude
Community

Home
Food
Family
Friends
Love
Food
Nature
Sun

Rainbows
Sourdough
Homeschool
Zoom

Time passing
Curves flattening
Priorities shifting
Divisions widening

Walks
Bubbles
Pubs
Schools?

Staying in
Looking out
Waiting for
A vaccine

Kerrie Farrar August 2020

Kerrie, Demie and Macey Farrar, Wales, UK

A printed piece of fabric appliquéd with cross and running stitches.

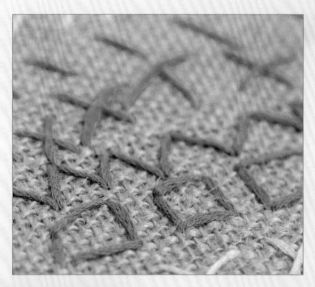

Kerrie, Demie and Macey Farrar,
Wales, UK

*These colourful squares were made by a family – lovely
to have some squares made by children.*

*One square includes a woven rainbow while the other
squares use the technique of appliqué. Straight, cross,
chain and running stitches all used.*

The dinosaur on your windowsill

This square represents a group set up on Facebook at the start of lockdown, 'The Dinosaur on Your Windowsill', by Dr Neil Gostling, Lecturer in Evolution and Palaebiology at Southampton University, UK. The group comprises experts in natural sciences and interested beginners. What makes the group special is the mantra 'There is no such thing as a daft question' and 'Keep it nice and friendly'. What has been amazing is the appetite and enthusiasm for the natural world and the exchange of ideas and comments, both within the group and across the world.

The square shows a feathered dinosaur, a modern interpretation of a Velociraptor, a member of a group of theropods which have evolved into birds. Also illustrated is an orange-tip butterfly (lots of butterfly enquiries answered by the group), a stag beetle (Britain's largest beetle and a local find in Hampshire), a snail, a ladybird (five spot) and a bumble bee. I have included the date as a nod to traditional embroideries and, being a museum natural scientist, data is very important!

The Dinosaur On Your Window Sill 2020

Christine Taylor, Hampshire, UK

Hand embroidered on Aida fabric with stranded cotton, using cross and turkey stitches.

My family

Covid-19 threw us all off balance. It's been a very strange time and I stitched my square at an angle to represent how everything has been skewed and nothing is following the path we thought it would at the beginning of 2020.

During this surreal time, my strength has come from being surrounded by my husband and daughters. I feel so fortunate for us to have been together in lockdown, able to support each other through the ups and downs of the uncertainty that has surrounded us. Olly, our mini Schnauzer, has given us all an immense amount of pleasure. As the old boy of the house, it's been lovely to have the time to do things at his pace. I'm not sure he'll appreciate the rush and tear of whatever the new normal brings.

Sadly the 300 miles between Mum and me, together with her vulnerable status, has made it tough. Thank goodness for technology, as well as her trusty band of friends and neighbours who have kept her going.

Thank you – two words that don't go nearly far enough to express our gratitude to those who selflessly threw themselves into helping all those in need. The colour of our chosen outfits, all shades of blue, is a tribute to those who work in the NHS. The sheer enormity of effort shown on the front line day after day in the battle against Covid-19 is something that I hope they never have to repeat in the future.

The borders of my square hold inside it precious togetherness, which I hope becomes part of everyone's new normal.

Mary Hewitt, London, UK

Hand embroidered using stranded cotton. French knots, back, stem, chain, blanket and straight stitches all used, with small areas of appliqué.

Masks and the internet

At the beginning of lockdown, I got the knitting needles out and started knitting a lap blanket. Just as I was finishing it, a Facebook page came up on my feed. Hearts for Hospitals was asking people to knit hearts, one to give to patients and one to the family who could not visit. They then asked for ear savers for nurses and later hats for premature babies and cuddle squares which Mum would wear and then leave with the baby. The ladies were all very eager and friendly, so I signed up.

From April till June we were flat out, getting through hundreds of buttons and the wool stash.

My square centre is a scrubs bag for nurses (I made 18), and around the four sides, ear savers which I lost count of. I only got to make two sets of hearts.

I had a routine during lockdown, which helped me keep sane. I found a freedom that I hadn't had for a long time, to do all the crafts I never found time for.

My day started with Mass on Facebook with my local church, followed by card making. I managed to make all the family and friends' cards up to October and around 50 Christmas cards. Then I found an embroidery Facebook page called textiles.org where artists set challenges each week and that stretched my skills to the max. One of the challenges was couching; hence why it is prominent in my square.

Facebook, Instagram and WhatsApp became a focus allowing me to share in like-minded people's work and to show my own. Where would we have been without the internet?

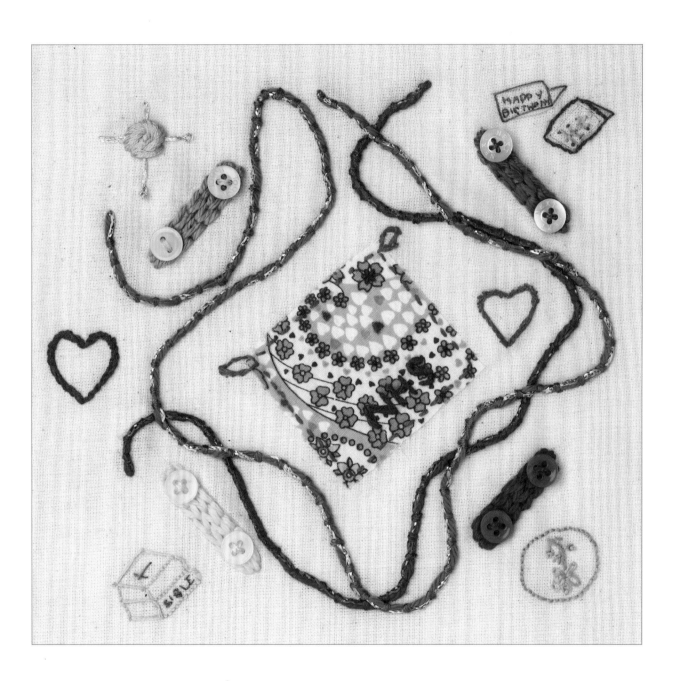

Eileen Galsworthy, London, UK

Hand embroidered using stranded cotton and metal threads. Buttons added for texture. Weaving stitches are used as well as straight, chain, back and couching stitches.

Rainbows of hope

I have really struggled to come up with a design, but I wanted to participate in this extraordinary project since I first heard Jill talk about it, on Jo Good's London Radio programme.

During the lockdown, I spent daytimes at home, in my garden and at my allotment, within my family's little bubble and surprisingly, even with two teens in the house, managed to get through the early days harmoniously. In the evenings, I would venture out on my own, for long walks on the eerily quiet car- and people-free streets. I saw that while the human world was in turmoil, the natural world, birds, insects, trees … all seemed to be thriving. From my home in North London, I saw colours in the spring skies, in the stars and the Moon, reminiscent of those I had seen in childhood, in my birthplace, Kenya.

These colours were beautifully represented in various colourful 'Rainbows of Hope' made by the neighbours' children and displayed on their windows to say 'thank you' to all the key workers living in the real world. The only glimpse most of us got of this was from the graphs and charts and slogans posted up on daily 5pm updates by the Government ministers. We all got consumed and lost in the data: the daily death count, the number of tests and infections. Inspired by these, I embroidered my own 'Rainbow of Hope' in April, practising stitches taught to me by my good friend, Yemii. Living in this surreal world, I had hope then that maybe in the long run, Covid-19's enforced slowing down of 21st-century life would lead us to reassess what's truly important: family, friends, nature and the environment. And also, to make us realise that, no matter who you are, or where you are, globally everyone is connected and somehow impacted by your own actions and inactions.

On 5 June 2020, I lost my younger cousin, Vishaal, aged 40. Covid-19 became a reality. We were very close. Our family's world fell apart… I have tried hard since to remain positive, but it is a daily struggle. Grief is hard at the best of times, but in a global pandemic and lockdown, it is harder still. You are unable to meet, hug and console family and friends in person, unable to meet and openly talk things through, unable to plan and have a fitting funeral and memorial service, unable to process all that has happened, unable to express all that is going on in your mind.

I do not know how long it will be before I can believe in 'Rainbows of Hope' again, but I want to envision positivity for myself, for my family and for my friends; and in Vishaal's memory, I have to believe that there is a light at the end of this long, dark tunnel. Writing this piece and putting this patch together for the Heroes Quilt has formed part of my grieving process.

Rami Shah, London, UK

Hand embroidered with stranded cotton. Appliqué and french knots, chain, back, stitch, running and lazy daisy stitches used.

Autumn stitches

Here I send you my contribution to such a beautiful project and a brief description of what it means to me.

I have grown up with seamstresses and the magic of creating with stitches, threads and textile fibres. Nature is my environment; it feeds my soul and nurtures my imagination.

From the need to merge my roots and my love for nature, 'Autumn Stitches' was born. It is my tribute to everything that once was and that still lasts in time, to traditions and to life.

This project was born in the month of March just when I began to recover from an oncological operation.

Immersing myself in it was the perfect treatment for my recovery and every stitch was a healing for my soul.

The original pieces are made with dried leaves collected in the fall. I have made an adaptation of the eco-print technique, printing the texture of a leaf; the stitches are similar to sashiko stitches, all of which complete the message.

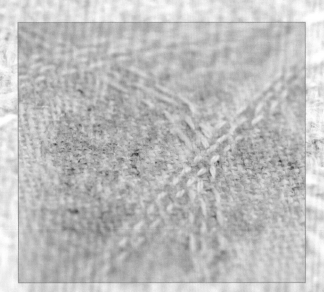

Sandra Guerra, Toledo, Spain

Printed using the eco-print technique and worked with cotton threads in running stitch.

Nightingale song sewing

The song of the nightingale drifted towards us like silk threads unravelling and then twisting and turning on the shimmering surface of the water. We live on a saltmarsh in Essex and my embroidery square was inspired by the memory of hearing a nightingale while kayaking with my husband Johannes in late spring 2020.

Nature forms an important source of emotional energy for me; this became especially obvious during the Covid-19 lockdown. Without the dulling and blanketing effect of anthropogenic noise from airplanes and traffic, listening to bird song became very intense. The day started with the dawn chorus, followed by a turtledove and a suite of other birds. At dusk, we were serenaded by a thrush and finally by the song of a nightingale. All this could be heard within a one-hour walk from home.

While in nature and observing biodiversity, I feel great hope for the future of our planet. I have used brightly coloured threads to symbolise this hope and the nightingale song.

A drone photograph, taken by, our son Leo, informed the image.

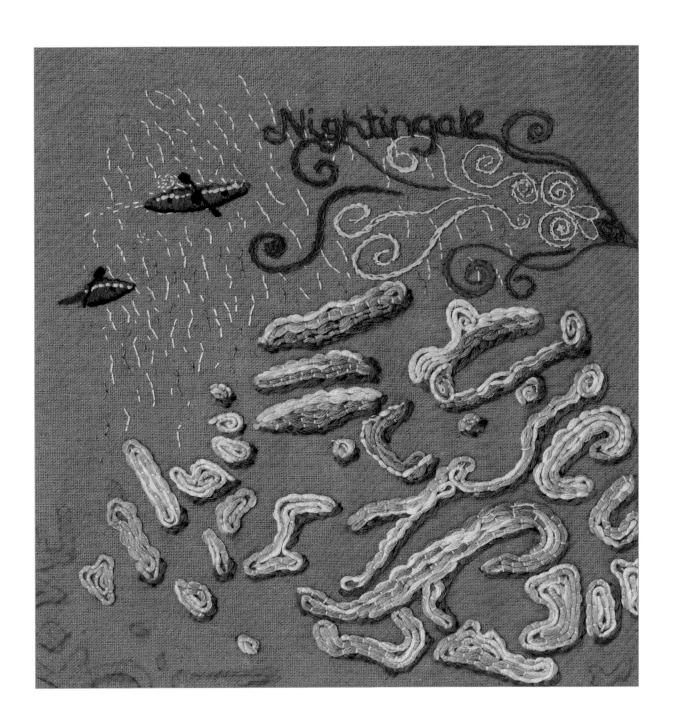

Sarah Darwin, Berlin, Germany

Hand embroidered using stranded cotton. Couching, stem, split, running and straight stitches used.

Bird song makes my heart sing

Thank you for encouraging and inspiring me to contribute a square for your Heroes Quilt project. I had not done any freestyle embroidery ever before – just a cross stitch kit many years ago. My lockdown story is the birds which have loudly accompanied our early walks in Highgate Woods. They have been louder than ever before: with the city being so quiet they've increased their volume. Ornithologists say that their new loudness means they are calling beyond their normal patch and competing with neighbours. Increased song volume apparently also makes birds fitter? It has been a positive to take from this strange time. The design of the bird on the cage came from a search of kits (Anchor) on the internet, but I've adapted it. It's been a great and strangely comforting experience.

Lucy Darwin, London, UK

Hand embroidered with soft cotton. Long-tailed french knots, chain, stem, back and running stitches used.

Lockdown spring 2020

How all our lives changed overnight! I am someone who worked from home and taught embroidery. I had a great routine of looking after my familiy's daily needs, running my small business and trying to keep fit. Suddenly it all changed. I found that we had a house full with all my daughters returning home and my sister-in-law coming to live with us.

I was very thankful to my pilates teacher Louise Taylor and my yoga teacher Helen Boby for their online classes. I found a new structure to my days. Louise was extremely quick about teaching three classes a week over Zoom. These classes became my lifeline. They gave me 'my time' and helped me to stay fit physically and mentally. At 12pm Louise's class would always 'freeze' and everyone would then spend the next few minutes telling Louise she was 'frozen'. This always made me laugh! My square shows a circle in the middle that represents a chalk circle, a pilates movement that Louise taught. It helped me focus on myself and think about my wellbeing, in what I think we all found to be a very difficult time. The ribbon square represents how we were all asked to stay at home and not venture out unless it was for our daily exercise or to go food shopping. We were all contained.

The flowers represent my garden and how much I treasured it more than ever and how nature just carried on regardless of the pandemic.

Jill Kipnis, London, UK

Hand embroidered using stranded cotton and silk ribbons. Stitches used are seeding, stem, french knots, running and stem and whipped stem. Silk ribbons used to create spider web roses, french knots and straight stitches.

'When life gives you limes, make them into margaritas!'

My embroidery is of two margaritas as my mum and I had so much fun making them during the lockdown. Every Friday evening, I would get the cocktail shaker out and rustle up some margaritas, while Mum ordered us an Indian takeaway – simple pleasures!

I also discovered that my local corner shop had huge crates of limes and there was never a queue, which made for a nice change compared to the Sainsbury's down the road.

I made sure to include a full lime at the bottom of the picture as I like the symbolism of citrus fruit being refreshing. Although it was a tough time for many people, I know a lot of us came out of lockdown feeling somewhat refreshed and recharged. It also made me think of the saying 'when life gives you lemons' – in this case, 'when life gives you limes, make them into margaritas!'

Kirsty Pym, London, UK

Hand embroidered using appliqué with blanket stitch. Straight, running, cross and chain stitches worked with stranded cotton.

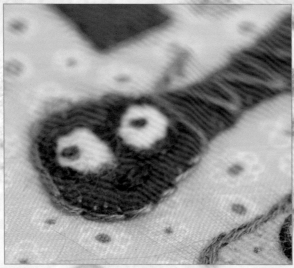

Wash your hands

I chose this design for a number of reasons. The message is what we have all been asked to do during the pandemic. Secondly, we have used our hands to wave to each other, clap for carers and be creative in lockdown. I wanted to add that as being a Christian has helped me cope with shielding and my prayers gave me comfort and strength, so I added the orange crosses. I did the word HANDS in rainbow colours as a tribute to the NHS, and the virus/germs I gave comical faces to defuse the fear that the pandemic has caused.

Judi Witcomb, Derby, UK

Hand embroidered using felt appliqué with stranded cotton. Stitches used are chain, straight, blanket and french knots.

Can you hear me now?

'Can you hear me now?' is the phrase I've heard, and said, more than any other this year. In Zoom calls as I try desperately to unmute myself, as someone's WiFi fails, as other household members fight for bandwidth. 'Can you hear me now? Can you hear me now?'

I realise how lucky we are to have technology that keeps us connected while we're separated. This year, we held a virtual Passover seder. The four of us around the dining table at home in Barnet were joined on Zoom by my sister and her family from Palmers Green, Mum in Hendon, my aunt and her boyfriend in Wales, and Nana (on my mobile phone – she doesn't have internet) in Snaresbrook.

We've celebrated birthdays over WhatsApp. I've chatted with my school friends – now scattered from Australia to Canada to Israel – more this year than in the last ten combined, the nine of us boxed in a screen like the Brady Bunch. I've even danced every Saturday night because a friend, who can't work as a DJ while the clubs are shut, runs his own personal dance party from his lounge, around the world.

I'm fortunate to have highlights from this year. For many, there has been overwhelming darkness. Unspeakable loss. Friends that couldn't be comforted. Goodbyes that couldn't be shared. Funerals that no-one could attend.

The world has changed this year, and this year has also shaped me. I see myself and those I love differently ... life seems more precious, more fragile. I am older, more tired, but more alive than before. So I scream into the static: 'Can you hear me now? Can you hear me now?'

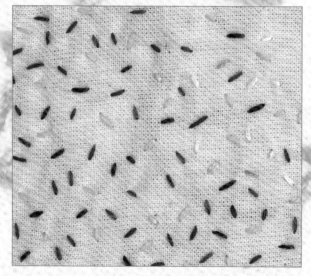

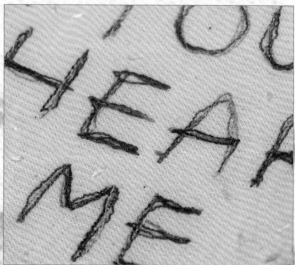

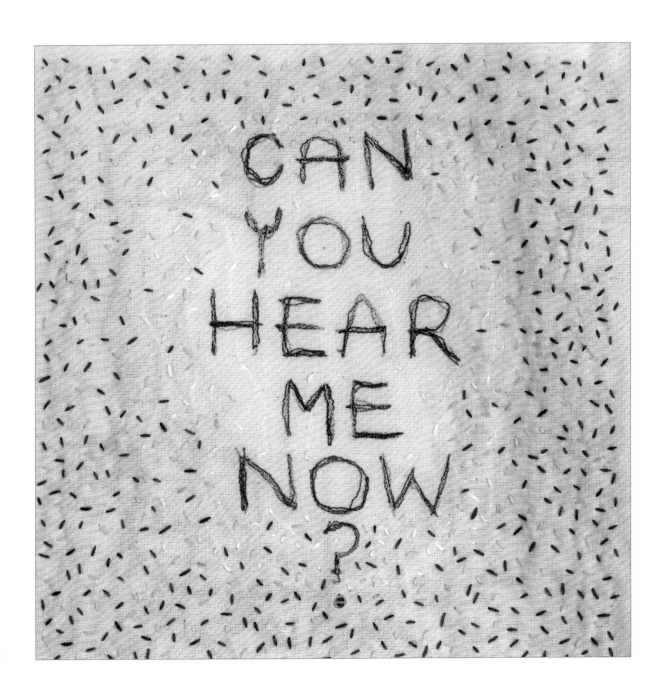

Hannah Lawrence, London, UK

Machine embroidered using free motion embroidery and filled with seeding stitch, using stranded cotton by hand.

My hero, my guitar

I love playing the guitar and singing, especially the great songs of the '60s. I had plenty of time to do that during the lockdown and have discovered quite a few old bands and songs on the internet that I have not heard of before. So I had great fun discovering new sounds from the era that took me away from the worries of what was going on around the world. The most important thing to me during the lockdown was having my family around. My daughters all came home and we had some wonderful family meals. I also learnt to embroider, and I was pleasantly surprised at how much I took to it.

Misha Kipnis, London, UK

Hand embroidered onto a printed background using felt appliqué with stab and stem stitches. Couched purl purl has been added for the strings of the guitar.

The simple pleasures of life

My family and our dog Snoopy kept me going during the lockdown. My 7-year- old boy, Snoopy our beagle – we walked a lot! My son learned to cycle without his training wheels; he mastered cycling! I walked and he cycled all around the neighbourhood. It was very comforting to be around nature. I am very grateful for good health, a roof over our heads and good food available all the time. I cooked a lot. And I got back to embroidering and cross stitch again. It gave me a sense of calm and peace. I made little embroidered articles and gifted them to friends and family. I cross stitched a little family portrait for my husband for Father's Day!

I feel the lockdown is a sign from the Almighty that we need to slow down and savour the simple pleasures that life offers.

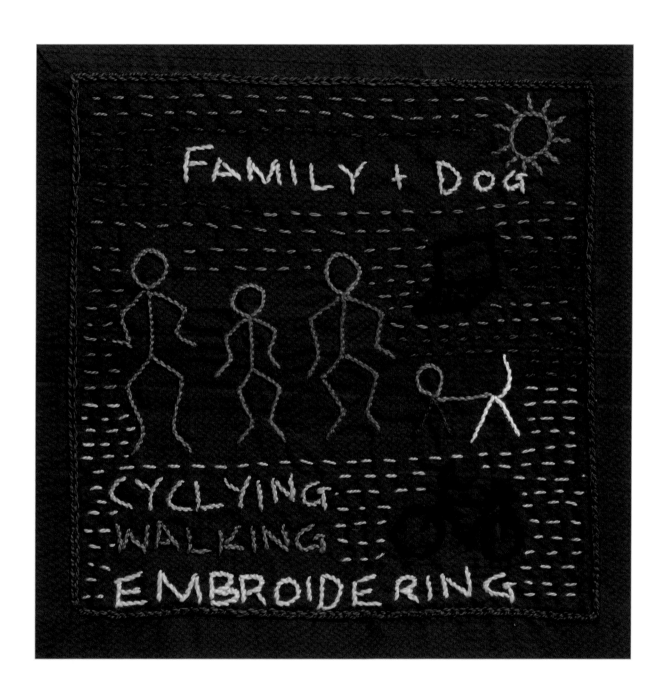

Pronita Roy Jaiswal, Texas, USA

Hand embroidered with perle thread using stem and running stitches.

My family

My parents brought my sisters and me up to understand the importance of family. Throughout this pandemic, my family have been my heroes as we have been supporting each other – laughing, crying, and giving advice.

My husband Phil and I have survived being in lockdown together. I have been grateful for the delicious meals he has cooked for me but not the weight I have put on!

I have two boys who are in their twenties. Matthew has worked from home and lives alone. He is part of our support bubble. It can be very lonely for people who are on their own. My other son James got a new job just before lockdown and moved into a flat to be closer to work. I was worried he might lose his job, plus have a large monthly rent to pay. But he passed the probation period and is doing well.

One of the highlights of the weekend is when we all get together to play online board games such as Cantan or Ticket to Ride. It seems a bit ironic, as when my boys were young, I spent so much time telling them to get off their computers as they were playing too many video games. Now I am asking them if they are free to play a game online at the weekend. It is a nice way to see them and keep in touch.

It can be extremely hard for a mother when she is told that she cannot hug or allow her child to come into the family home. But it is important that we comply with the rules to keep people safe.

All my sisters and I keep in touch by WhatsApp on our phones. We send funny pictures, videos and texts to check on each other and to make sure our families are keeping well.

My sister Sally volunteers at Citizens Advice, helping people with benefit enquiries. She has had to learn to do this online and then spends a long time writing reports of what she has advised. Sadly, she lost her dog Gypsy during lockdown but has managed to get a rescue dog. Taking the dog for walks every day helps to keep her spirits up.

Margaret's husband Malcolm sadly died during the lockdown though it was not due to Covid-19. She was fortunate that she was able to be at his bedside when he died, as during this time so many people have died alone.

My sister Diana has worked throughout the pandemic at a school providing meals for children of key workers and vulnerable children. When the country clapped for the NHS and key workers on a Thursday night at 8 o'clock, I always did a little clap for her too.

I feel incredibly lucky to have such a great family and so enormously proud of my boys. So, a big thank you to all my heroes.

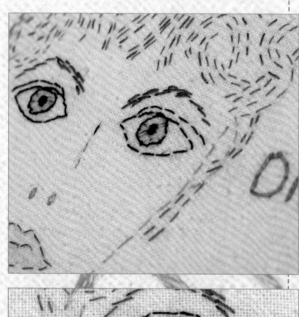

Sally   Phil

James   Diana

Matthew   Margaret

My Family

Paula Bradbury, London, UK

Hand embroidered using running, back and couching stitches in stranded cotton. The lips are carefully coloured in using textile paint.

Home is where the heart is

After spending more time at home than ever before, the inspiration for my embroidery is 'Home is where the heart is' and I have chosen my lovely garden to reflect this.

Spring was stressful – hearing that Covid-19 was spreading fast across the globe, we thought in March our daughter and her partner would be stranded in South America while backpacking. (Happily they managed to get home – she's still here and despite the challenges of living at home with parents again it's been wonderful!)

Then came lockdown, so we isolated ourselves, walking and cycling for exercise, only going out shopping for food every 3–4 weeks (shopping online was impossible), worrying about panic buying and not finding what we needed on the shelves – loo rolls, pasta, flour, yeast (trying to keep busy we threw ourselves into baking ... banana cake became a favourite). We 'binge watched' TV, and started crafting again. I joined a local group making scrubs and face masks for NHS workers unable to source the extras they urgently needed – good to feel useful. And the nation started clapping on Thursday nights to show our appreciation of NHS frontline workers: true heroes in all this chaos.

No longer going out to work and not seeing friends and family was difficult for us all. I missed seeing my sons, who live miles away from home. Our holiday abroad was cancelled, and after weeks of uncertainty, our daughter's wedding was postponed ... hopefully to happen next year.

Then summer arrived early. The sun shone, we had weeks of glorious weather and began to enjoy being at home.

Our garden especially has been a place for us all to relax, feel safe and appreciate what we are so lucky to have. I loved sitting in the sunshine with my daughter by the pond with a good book or our embroidery, listening to the birds and watching as they reared their young – magpies and pigeons, the thrush that nested in the roof, and a cheeky robin which often joins me while I'm gardening. We enjoyed watching butterflies and bees feeding on colourful flowers, and dragonflies flitting across our pond (the first of the many garden 'projects' that have kept my husband

busy – and happy – all summer). He's also replaced fencing, built an amazing compost bin using recycled wood, reshaped the borders and repaired the house roof.

We've watched our cat Bella snoozing in sunny spots and have played garden games again – badminton over the washing line, boules and swingball. We planted seeds – every packet we could find, even though many didn't grow! And we have harvested strawberries, lettuce, potatoes, tomatoes, peppers and lots of beans.

We feel so lucky that we have had our lovely garden as a place of refuge during this time of uncertainty. Home really is where our heart is and I hope this is reflected in my embroidery.

P. S. We finally got to see our two sons and their partners recently and it gave us the best feeling ever!

Teresa Evans, Chester, UK

Hand embroidered with organza appliqué using stranded cotton. French knots, back, straight and lazy daisy stitches used.

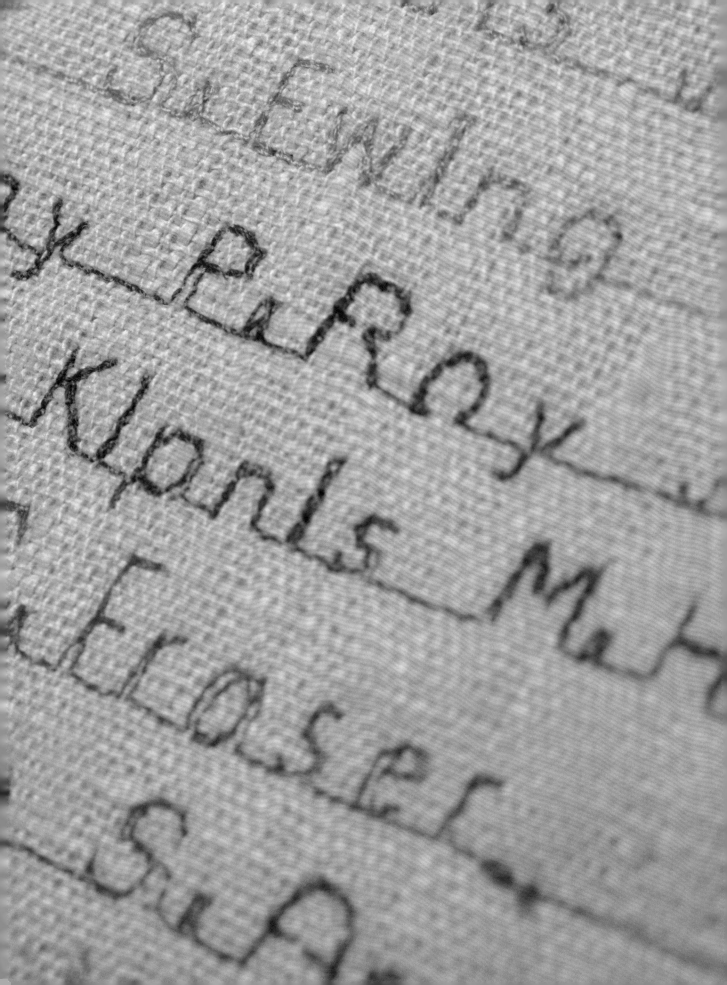

The Makers

Embroidered using a Bernina sewing machine on linen with machine embroidery thread.

Thank you to all.

The Final Square

Reverse appliqué with a hand-dyed silk backing fabric, machine embroidered using machine embroidery thread.

A simple square to remind generations to come what the quilt is called and how it came about during the spring lockdown of 2020, due to the worldwide Covid-19 pandemic.

Acknowledgements

I would like to say thank you so much to everyone who sent squares and stories to be included in the Heroes Quilt. The trust that people gave to Sue and me in delivering this project has been terrific.

I would also like to say thank you to my photographer, Michael Wicks, for his remarkable photographs and help in formatting the book. His work really helps the embroidered squares come alive.

Thank you to Jill Collins and Chris Fraser for helping with the editing, greatly appreciated.

Thanks you to Paula Bradbury for helping me sew the quilt together – before lockdown number two!

Thank you textile.org as they were great at letting me place a post about the project on their social media site. It so helped to spread the word and also BBC Radio London, the Jo Good Show, where I was interviewed about the idea at a very early stage.

My final thank you is to Sue Arran. If Sue had not phoned me back at the beginning of the spring lockdown, this project would never have happened. I have so enjoyed putting it all together and helping people create something historical in stitch, with Sue being there every step of the way.